Buying Gemstones and Jewellery in
GREAT BRITAIN

First Edition

Kim Rix GG (GIA)

Published by
Filament Publishing Ltd
16, Croydon Road, Waddon, Croydon,
Surrey, CR0 4PA, United Kingdom
Telephone +44 (0)20 8688 2598
Fax +44 (0)20 7183 7186
info@filamentpublishing.com
www.filamentpublishing.com

© Kim Rix 2021

The right of Kim Rix to be identified as the author of this work
has been asserted by her in accordance with the
Designs and Copyright Act 1988.

ISBN 978-1-913623-48-7

Printed by PrintGuy

This book is subject to international copyright and may not be copied
in any way without the prior written permission of the publishers.

Foreword

*"This sceptred isle, This earth of majesty...
This blessed plot, this earth, this realm."*

One of Britain's most famous exports, William Shakespeare got it right when he thus described his home country in his play *Richard II*. Whilst Britain's cultural heritage is known around the world, Britain is so much more. Yes, we have the history and the heritage, the country houses and market towns dating back centuries, but we also have a diverse and modern family of islands including a truly global capital in London that reflects our magpie nation, vibrant cities with world-class theatre and music scenes. And if you fancy something delicious, we do more than fish and chips, having a vibrant food and drink scene with some of the best produce in the world.

Whether it's *Harry Potter*, *Paddington Bear* or *Game of Thrones*, you can visit where films and TV shows have been made and where they were inspired. Or feel the buzz of a sporting event – many sports were invented here, so what better than to cheer on your favourite team in your favourite sport – from horseracing and tennis, to cricket, football or rugby?

The landscapes will amaze – from the rolling hills of England, the fire and stone of Wales' castles and the awe-inspiring Highlands of Scotland. Whilst we may not be the home of sapphires and rubies, there are plenty of jewels woven into our rich tapestry of a nation.

Any trip around Britain really shouldn't be limited to our wonderful capital, London – there is so much more to experience across the whole of our small land. Wherever you go, you can be assured of a warm welcome.

Historic culture meets modern culture in a mix that is as compelling as it is unique. The only question you need to ask is, how am I going to fit it all in?!

Joss Croft
CEO
UKinbound
The voice of inbound tourism
www.ukinbound.org

Fluorite from the Diana Maria mine, Weardale © Kim Rix

Contents

Background — 7
- Why you need this book — 9
- What makes me an expert? — 10

Buying gemstones and jewellery — 11
- The four types of gemstone — 16
- Three things you need to know — 19
- Deciding what you want — 20
- Choosing where to buy — 22
- About Whitby jet — 24
- Tips for identifying jet — 36
- About amber — 40
- About Blue John — 48
- Other gemstones and minerals found in Great Britain — 56
- Welsh gold — 75
- Scottish gold — 80
- Gold panning — 81
- Museums with gemstone and mineral collections — 83
- Famous British treasure hoards — 94
- Tourist attractions — 95
- How to become a gemstone collector — 97
- Rules and regulations of rock hunting — 99
- Associations and Academies in Great Britain — 103
- Clubs and societies — 104
- How to find a jeweller — 106
- Questions to ask when buying jewellery — 107
- How to make a complaint — 108

Essential Information 111
- Certificates of authenticity and grading reports 112
- Where to get your gemstones tested 113
- Jewellery shopping 114
- Importing and exporting 115
- Recommended books and useful links 118

Appendices 121
- Glossary 122
- Acknowledgements 125
- About the author 126
- Disclaimer 126
- Connect with us 127

BACKGROUND

Cornish Turquoise © *Two Skies, Scotland*

BACKGROUND

Why you need this book

This book is an essential tourist guide to gemstones in Great Britain. It is a 'how to' manual for hobbyists, frequent travellers and those already in the jewellery trade with little knowledge about British gemstones. I have written it to help you feel more confident about the buying process.

The gem trade is rather a secretive industry and this is as true in Britain as anywhere else in the world. There's a vast array of myths, inaccuracies and very deliberate deceptions out there, but don't let that put you off – my clear and jargon-free guidance will allow you to navigate your gemstone buying journey with ease.

Whether you are hoping to treat yourself to an extra-special souvenir of your latest adventure, buying supplies for your jewellery-making venture or travelling to learn more about the gemstone industry, what could be more exciting than buying your gemstone in the very country whose earth formed it?

This book will give you the vital information you need before making your purchase. In it, I disclose what websites don't tell you.

I'll reveal:

Who to trust
What to look for
When to walk away
Where to look
Why you need to be sure

What makes me an expert?

It has taken 2681 miles and a few calculated risks to gain the knowledge I'm going to share with you. Everything in this book is based on personal experience and local expertise.

The letters after my name are testament to my knowledge. I'm a gemmologist with qualifications from the GIA (Gemological Institute of America) – the world's leading authority on gemstones. However, it's my extensive travel and research that will make this book so useful to you.

A private collection of Blue John artefacts © *Kim Rix*

BUYING GEMSTONES AND JEWELLERY IN GREAT BRITAIN

BUYING GEMSTONES AND JEWELLERY IN **GREAT BRITAIN**

Before we begin, I'd like to add a little note for readers unfamiliar with the different names we have for these little islands! **Great Britain** (or simply, Britain) refers to the land mass of **England, Scotland** and **Wales** (in this case, along with their associated islands). That's the scope of this book.

The United Kingdom is a political term referring to these countries plus Northern Ireland. The British Isles is a geographical term that encompasses both Great Britain and the whole island of Ireland.

Britain has one of the longest histories of mining in the world and was at the forefront of the mining industry during the industrial revolution. There is a wealth of world-class mineral specimens to be found. Unlike parts of south-east Asia, though, Britain is not rich in the world's best-known gemstones, nor is it a destination for cheap gemstone bargains. Sapphire, beryl, ruby and even diamond have been unearthed in Britain, but these findings are extraordinarily rare and newsworthy events. In fact, the mere possibility of Scottish diamonds nearly sparked a diamond rush in 1999.

However, Britain has some interesting and beautiful native gemstones that are more readily available and deserve wider appreciation. For the jewellery enthusiast, there are hundreds of jewellery shops, some fantastic museums and good beaches for treasure hunting!

Outer Hebrides, Isle of Harris and Lewis © Kim Rix

BUYING GEMSTONES AND JEWELLERY

The four types of gemstone

There are four categories of gemstone you need to be aware of:

1. Natural, untreated gemstones
Top of the range are natural, untreated gemstones. 'Natural' means they were formed in the earth and 'untreated' means they have not had anything done to enhance their beauty besides being cut and set. Because of their rarity, these can cost thousands of pounds and you should expect them to come with a lab report.

2. Natural gemstone but treated
Next in line are treated stones. In the grand scheme of things, 95% of all gemstones sold have been treated in some way, but the figure is closer to 99% for stones such as rubies and sapphires.

Heating is the most common gemstone treatment, but other treatments may be used to enhance appearance. These include bleaching (e.g. pearls and jadeite jade), dying (e.g. pearls, emerald, ruby) and oiling (e.g. emeralds).

3. Synthetic or created gemstones
The term 'synthetic' properly refers to a stone with the same physical and chemical properties as a natural stone, but which was created in a lab rather than in the earth.

Confusingly, some people use the term 'synthetic' interchangeably with 'simulated', which means 'fake'. Always make sure you know what you're buying! True synthetic (created) stones are not always cheaper than a natural stone – it depends on the quality of the stone in question and how easy it is to produce in a lab.

BUYING GEMSTONES AND JEWELLERY

Buyer beware! 'Amber' with lizard inside (but it's probably plastic) © Kim Rix

Many people prefer synthetic stones because they have fewer inclusions and their carbon footprint can be smaller than stones mined using industrial machinery. Others believe that synthetic stones lack the interest, history and romance of a gemstone formed underground over billions of years. The best decision is the one that feels right for you!

4. Imitation or simulation gemstone

Imitations or simulations are fakes – a cheaper material made to look like a more expensive gem. Fake doesn't always mean the stone is glass, however – it might be a less valuable gemstone sold as a more expensive one. For example, garnet is sometimes sold as ruby and iolite as sapphire.

The above applies to all types of gemstone that you might find in a British jeweller's shop – both imported gemstones and those mined in Great Britain.

The gemstone information in this book will give you a good head start, but you need to keep in mind that even experts can't always make an accurate identification with just their naked eye.

You can – and should – have your gemstone tested before you hand over significant money, even if it already has a certificate of authenticity or 'written guarantee'. This is simply a piece of paper confirming that your gemstone is real, according to the seller. However, anyone can write a certificate!

A laboratory identification report goes into more detail about the stone. If you do want to get a proper report for your gemstone, you can visit a reputable gem lab.

BUYING GEMSTONES AND JEWELLERY

Three things you need to know

1. Different areas in England, Scotland and Wales have different rockhounding rules – always check.

2. SSSI / Geoparks – Gem hunters should be aware that several parks and other areas in Great Britain are now protected as **Sites of Special Scientific Interest (SSSI).** If so, you're not allowed to remove anything from them.

   'Right to roam' legislation in Scotland is very liberal, although restrictions are tighter when it comes to digging. Problems always arise when finds are made of precious materials with substantial value. Conflicts of interest, as well as ownership, arise. This has been particularly true of Scottish pearls and Scottish sapphires, which are now subject to very strict legislation.

3. You can export jewels, gold and precious metals without a licence or certificate, except for uncut diamonds.

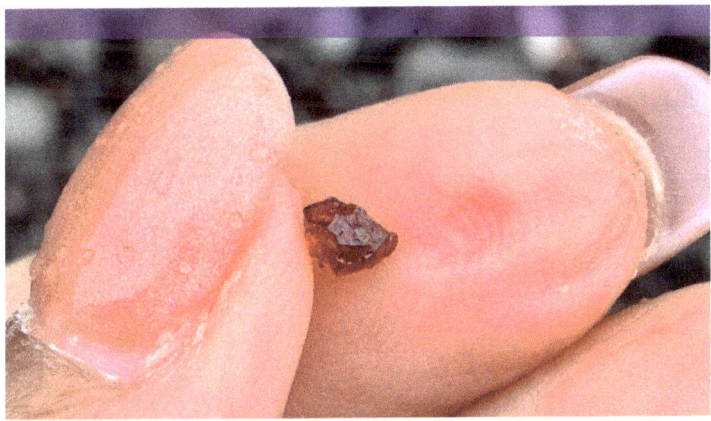

A garnet found on Elie beach (Ruby Bay) © Kim Rix

BUYING GEMSTONES AND JEWELLERY IN **GREAT BRITAIN**

Deciding what you want

There are a few questions you need to ask yourself before purchasing:

Loose stone or set?
If you can't find a piece of ready-made jewellery that suits your taste, why not buy a loose gemstone on your travels? There are many jewellers in Great Britain who will be able to set your stone in jewellery for you, so you might want to take it home for your preferred local jeweller to do the job.

What's the stone for?
Are you intending to set your gemstone in a ring, a brooch, a bracelet, a necklace? Think about the how the size and cut of your gemstone will affect the look of the piece. Whether buying a loose gemstone or a finished piece, make sure you consider the toughness of the gemstone. A soft gemstone won't last very long in an everyday ring.

How much do I want to spend?
This is important. You need to decide on a budget before you approach anywhere that sells gemstones. It's easy to get carried away and spend more than you can really afford.

How do I want to pay?
How you want to pay will affect where you buy. You should use a credit card, as this will offer you some level of protection against fraud.

Where do I want to do my gemstone shopping?
Knowing your budget and how you want to pay should determine where you should buy: at a large and established jewellery shop, at a jewellery or mineral show, in a museum, at a small gemstone merchant/trader or at auction. Let's look at those options more closely...

BUYING GEMSTONES AND JEWELLERY

Take a walk in Ganllwyd. It's a beautiful part of Wales. Visit the falls of Rhaedr Ddu and discover the remote remnants of a bygone goldrush. © Kim Rix

Choosing where to buy

Option 1: buying from a shop
It's more advisable for a tourist who is inexperienced in gemstones to buy from a reputable shop or brand. If there is any issue with a shop-bought gemstone, you can more easily go back to the place to complain.

For a gemstone or piece of jewellery, think about the kind of establishment you are in. A shop or dealer with a reputation to uphold will have a real and serious interest in selling you genuine goods.

Famous jewellery shopping areas in Great Britain include Hatton Garden in London and The Jewellery Quarters in Birmingham.

Option 2: buying at a jewellery or mineral show
There are no gemstone-specific outdoor street markets or gem shows for the general public in Great Britain, though you'll find stalls dedicated to crystals and minerals in local markets and craft fairs.

Serious mineral collectors will find it's best to buy from a shop or at auction.

Britain hosts relatively few mineral shows. The best one is the Bakewell Rock Exchange in Derbyshire. It's a two-day event organised by the Peak Lapidary and Mineral Society.

You can find more shows listed at:

www.rockngem.co.uk
www.mineralandfossilevents.co.uk
www.ruralmagpie.co.uk/pages/rural-magpie-fairs
www.beadworkersguild.org.uk

Option 3: buying from a gem museum

Great Britain is awash with gem museums. They are hidden gems (pun intended!) but you may pay over the odds in their gift shops, though, as they're usually priced for tourism.

 Top Tip: The one to watch out for in gift shops is opalite, which is often sold in the gemstone section. It's a convincing lookalike for Sri Lankan moonstone and opal, but is actually glass!

Opalite glass © Kim Rix

Option 4: buying at auction

The most famous auction houses in the UK are Bonhams and Christie's. Don't be put off by their aristocratic associations, though – you don't necessarily need to have deep pockets to buy at auction here.

The serious collector of gemstones and minerals can find some stunning specimens at Summers Place Auctions: www.summersplaceauctions.com/auction/search

Option 5: buying on recommendations

A personal recommendation from people you trust is a powerful thing. If you have friends, colleagues or contacts in Great Britain, use them.

In this section, you'll find Britain's most famous native gemstones – Whitby jet, Baltic amber and Blue John.

About Whitby jet

Whitby jet, the 'Jewel of North Yorkshire', is a gemstone created when driftwood is subjected to extreme pressure over millions of years.

We cannot measure jet on the Mohs scale of hardness because it is not a **homogenous** material. However, we can say that it is soft – a little softer than fluorite.

Jet is found in several countries, including China, Siberia, Germany and Spain, but the world's finest quality comes from the pretty North Yorkshire location of Whitby – a seaside town immortalised in Bram Stoker's famous novel as the landing place of Count Dracula and now home to the Whitby Goth Festival.

Jet is arguably Britain's oldest natural resource and is culturally important to the identity of the British people.

Jet has long been seen as a magical material, probably due to its mirror-like shine and the static charge it acquires. In Britain, jet was carved throughout the Neolithic and Bronze Ages, before falling out of favour in the Iron Age. The arrival of the Romans in Britain saw jet become popular again, thanks to their belief that it protected its wearer from the evil eye.

Jet became hugely fashionable in the 19th century, when it was officially designated a stone of mourning after the death of George IV in 1830. Queen Victoria cemented its popularity during the latter half of the 19th century when, bereaved of her beloved husband Prince Albert, she remained in formal mourning for her last forty years, wearing the gemstone in her jewellery. Known for its remarkably high **lustre** when polished, Whitby jet made a fitting mourning gemstone for a queen and anyone who was anyone wanted to emulate her.

At the height of its fashion, it is believed there were up to 300 jet mines in North Yorkshire. Traces of these can still be seen, though it is now illegal to mine jet and highly dangerous even to enter a disused mine. I strongly advise that you do not even think of doing so!

Jet brooch and earrings © Kim Rix

A Whitby jet cameo of Queen Victoria, carved by John Speedy © Kim Rix

Collectors have traditionally combed the beach looking for jet washed up with the tide, or prised it out of the shale cliffs on the shoreline. Please note it is illegal to take jet from the cliffs. They are highly unstable and have claimed lives over the years, so please stay away from them!

If you're keen to hunt for your own piece of jet, you'll need to look for 'sea-washed' jet – the kind that's found on the beach itself. However, jet is not easy for a beginner to identify and can be confused with all sorts of other substances that wash up on the shoreline.

Firstly, it's important to note that jet is a generic term that covers any sort of black, Victorian jewellery. There is still no Trading Standards law relating to the sale of genuine Whitby jet and so it is very much a case of 'caveat emptor' – let the buyer beware.

BUYING GEMSTONES AND JEWELLERY

So what do you need to look out for if you want a genuine piece of Whitby jet?

Whilst writing this book, I drove to Whitby to talk to Sarah Steele, a jet researcher with four decades of experience in collecting Whitby jet. Sarah's knowledge about the identification of jet simulants, collecting on the beach and her tips for recognising jet have been an immense help in the preparation of this section.

There are three categories of Whitby jet simulants that you need to be aware of: natural simulants, man-made simulants and imported jet posing as Whitby jet. Some of the man-made simulants aren't produced any more and will only be found in antique Victorian jewellery. Many of them will have their own appeal – bakelite jewellery, for example, is popular with collectors and fans of vintage jewellery. It's not genuine Whitby jet, though!

1. Natural simulants:
Black gemstones, including:
Black amber (almost identical to Whitby jet), shungite, black obsidian, black coral, black diamond, black sapphire, haematite and onyx.

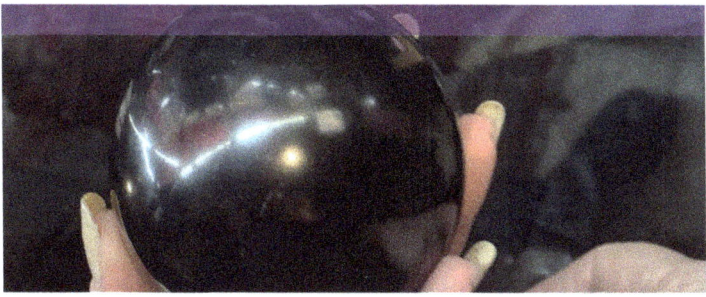

Shungite – a jet simulant © Kim Rix

Blackened amber (smaller bracelet) vs jet (larger bracelet) © Kim Rix

Dark wood, such as bog oak and ebony
Bog oak was never intended to be a jet simulant, simply to celebrate the Irish crafts movement. Ebony is a dense dark brown/black hardwood, famous for its use on piano keyboards.

2. Man-made simulants
It's important to note that the Victorians would sell anything remotely plastic-like and black as Whitby jet. Nowadays, technology is more advanced and modern plastics can be indistinguishable if you are not an expert.

BUYING GEMSTONES AND JEWELLERY

Pressed horn or tortoiseshell

The earliest jet simulant was animal horn – heated, dyed and pressed into moulds. Despite predating the jet industry by over a century, pressed horn is still arguably one of the best simulants of Whitby jet – it looks convincing to a non-expert and has a shelf life of approximately 500 years.

Vulcanite

Vulcanite (vulcanised rubber) was probably the most extensively produced jet simulant. It was made from rubber and sulphur, which form a hard biopolymer when mixed together. When new it was black enough to be mistaken for jet, though not as lustrous. It gradually becomes more of a khaki colour once exposed to sunlight.

Dyed pressed horn – a convincing jet simulant © Kim Rix

Vulcanite – a jet simulant © Kim Rix

Bois Durci

Bois Durci, invented in 1855, was an early form of plastic made from cow's blood mixed with powdered wood and dye. It ranges from brown to dark brown/black in colour.

French jet

French jet is simply cut black glass. Nobody knows why it's called French jet, as it was made in the UK. You'll tend to see it on jewellery in the form of small beads.

A cameo carved from Bois Durci © Kim Rix

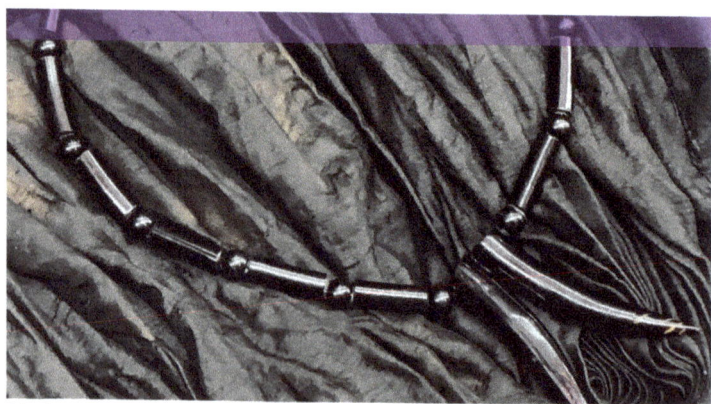

Black coral necklace – a jet simulant © Kim Rix

Vauxhall glass
Often sold as jet, Vauxhall glass is similar to French jet, but with the addition of a mirror backing on the piece to give it more lustre. Sometimes it's really dark cranberry or blue.

Bakelite
Bakelite is the trade name for phenol formaldehyde resin. Discovered in 1907, bakelite was the first recorded fully synthetic polymer and was lightweight and lustrous enough to be a serious competitor for Whitby jet.

Galalith
Galalith was the commercial name for an early biopolymer made from milk and formaldehyde. When dyed black, it was a convincing Whitby jet simulant.

Celluloid cellulose nitrate
Discovered in 1862, celluloid cellulose nitrate is another common simulant of jet. It's a man-made plastic, better known for its use in the production of ping-pong balls.

Papier mâché
Even papier mâché can make a good simulant when painted and varnished.

3. Imported jet
At the height of the Victorian jet industry, manufacturers imported many tonnes of jet from Spain. Unfortunately the jet they imported wasn't Spain's finest and was not as stable in the damp, British climate as genuine Whitby jet.

Reconstituted jet necklace © *Kim Rix*

Nowadays, jet from Mongolia, Georgian Republic and China is sold raw for jewellery making and finished as beads.

Mongolian jet necklace © *Kim Rix*

Top Tip: The safest way to buy genuine Whitby jet is through local dealers who collect and process the jet themselves.

Collecting jet on the beach

Plenty of materials wash up on Whitby's beaches that an amateur collector might easily mistake for jet. These include shale, burnt wood, coal, rubber, tar and even bat droppings! Not everything that's black is jet.

Where to look:

Jet has the same **specific density** as seaweed, which means they tend to wash in together. Follow your nose to the piles of rotting seaweed on the beach!

The streak test:

The easiest way for an amateur to discard some of the lookalikes is by doing the 'streak test'. For this, you will need some sandpaper suitable for wet and dry sanding. It should be super fine in grade and light in colour. Gently rub the material back and forth on the sandpaper and study the colour of the streak it leaves behind.

- If you have found hard Whitby jet (i.e. the kind you're looking for) the streak will be a light, brownish orange (the colour of powdered ginger).

- Soft Whitby jet is not usually used for jewellery, but it will leave a darker brown streak (the colour of chocolate).

- Coal, charcoal and burnt wood will leave a black or very dark streak.

- Plastic, shale and other stones will leave a white or grey streak.

BUYING GEMSTONES AND JEWELLERY IN **GREAT BRITAIN**

A view of the ruined Gothic Whitby Abbey, Yorkshire © Kim Rix

BUYING GEMSTONES AND JEWELLERY

Tips for identifying jet

1. Jet is warm, whereas glass and stone feel cool on your skin.

2. Jet is light – lighter than glass or stone. If placed in a cup of water, it will sink slowly.

3. Jet is just hard enough not to give when you try to dig your nail into it (unlike tar).

4. If what you're looking at has brown, greenish or grey tones, it's not jet.

5. It's not possible to screw into jet, so if the jewellery's fixings are screwed in, it's not jet.

6. Jet is carved, not moulded, so look for carving marks and any telltale signs of moulding.

7. Jet jewellery will almost always be polished on the back as well as the front. Turn the piece over. If it has lathe marks or a rough surface, it's almost certainly not jet.

8. Bubbles or pitting in the material suggest either glass or reconstituted jet. Reconstituted jet is made from powdered Georgian jet mixed with resin.

BUYING GEMSTONES AND JEWELLERY

9 It's rare to find Whitby jet necklaces with same-sized beads. Real Victorian jet necklaces tend to have graduated beads.

10 Victorian jet man-made simulants often have an odd smell. Depending on the material, it could smell sulphurous, milky or like formaldehyde, for example.

© Kim Rix

Jet testing

If you do an internet search on testing for jet, you'll probably find references to the hot needle test. DON'T DO IT! Nothing devalues an item more than destroying it.

Best way to clean jet?

Jet attracts grease and dirt, hence can be difficult to clean. Jet likes water, so you can get it wet.

CAUTION: It's generally safe to use an ultrasonic cleaner with present-day genuine jet jewellery, but they are best avoided for antiques. If the item is a Victorian simulant, ultrasound can weaken the glue and even (in some cases) totally destroy the piece. Even with genuine jet antique items, the glue could still be weakened and damaged.

How much do you pay for jet?

Unlike other gemstones, jet is not sold by carat weight. Manufacturers buy jet by the pound, then the retail price depends on the size of the piece and the amount of work put in. The price might also reflect exceptional sizes and the era – pieces made in the 1880's are valuable. Because of jet's scarcity, it is typically expensive.

 Top tip: Don't buy jet online on sites like eBay or Etsy and expect to get real jet.

Worth a visit: Museum of WhitbyJet, to see the world's largest Whitby jet specimen.

Visit: www.museumofwhitbyjet.com

BUYING GEMSTONES AND JEWELLERY

Comparing vulcanite (left) and Whitby jet (right) © Kim Rix

About amber

Amber is the fossilized resin of long-extinct trees, and hence categorized as an organic gemstone. Amber comes from a type of pine *(Pinus Succinifera)* that produced large amounts of resin, which would run down the tree through its bark, often trapping insects and plants as it flowed. With the beginning of the Ice Age, the resin became trapped under ice and hardened under the extreme pressure and temperature.

Amber occurs in different colours, the most common being a brownish orange, followed by green. Rarer colours include red and blue. Amber may also be heated or dyed to improve the appearance and colour of the stone. As amber is an organic material, it is constantly oxidising so its colour darkens over time.

Genuine amber with mosquito trapped inside © Kim Rix

Opaque amber is caused by thousands and thousands of microscopic air bubbles trapped inside it when it was still a resin. Then, under the pressure of the ice, stress marks formed, which made the piece completely opaque. It is estimated that there can be over 20,000 microscopic air bubbles per cubic centimetre in a single piece of opaque amber.

Certain inclusions in amber are considered desirable and this is because they are often of great scientific and archaeological interest. An amber pendant may contain, for example, a fossilized prehistoric insect or plant.

Deposits of amber can be found all over the world, though the best-known

A stunning amber specimen © Kim Rix

amber is Baltic amber. In Britain, Baltic amber occasionally washes up on the north-east coast of Scotland, but the best places to look are on the Norfolk coast and the beaches of Southwold in Suffolk. This is thanks to the slowly moving ice sheets of the most recent ice age, which collected amber from the forests that covered what is now the Baltic Sea and deposited it on the shoreline around England's east coast.

England and Scotland are home to amber that is typically 40-60 million years old. The oldest British amber found was over 100 million years

Amber Buddha from the Amber Shop & Museum, Southwold © Kim Rix

old, found in Northumberland. One very famous and outstanding amber specimen resides in the National Museum of Scotland.

Other known sources of amber include Indonesia, Mexico, South America, Dominica Republic and Burma. This amber is sent to the Baltics (Poland, Lithuania, Latvia and Estonia) to be crafted into jewellery and other ornaments. Because amber is so soft and brittle, crafting is done by hand rather than using electronic machinery.

Beachcombing for amber in Britain

If you'd like to try your luck at finding your own piece of amber, the coastline between Felixstowe and Southwold in East Suffolk is known as the 'Amber Coast'. In Norfolk, try the Groyne at Waxham Horsey on the Eccles coast: go to the far end of the beach, beyond the last sea defence. Another place to try is Sidestrand Beach in Cromer.

As with searching for jet on Whitby's beaches, you'll need to take precautions. Make sure you know the tide times, take appropriate clothing and accessories for the weather and make sure someone knows where you will be.

Look for pieces of amber on the beach © Kim Rix

Types of fakes

Unfortunately, there are many amber simulants in the shops today. These are the most common:

Reconstituted amber: small waste pieces of amber that have been melted down, mixed with plastic and moulded. Necklaces usually have large oval or barrel shaped beads that are red in colour and cloudy.

Top tip: look for a moulded pattern – it's subtly different from the patterns found in genuine amber.

Pressed amber: amber cut offs, pressed together under extreme pressure. Pressed amber was considered fake for a long time but nowadays, because nothing else has been added, it is regarded as amber and sold with a certificate of authenticity. Let the buyer beware!

Amber glass: A mixture of sand, soda ash and limestone, heated to a very high temperature.

Bakelite: heavily used to simulate both jet and amber in the Victorian age, bakelite is a plastic made from synthetic components. Bakelite 'amber' beads are usually clear and reddish in colour.

Copal: This is very young amber – not (yet) fossilized and from a much more recent era. It's not legal to sell copal as amber.

BUYING GEMSTONES AND JEWELLERY

How to spot a fake amber

- Plastic amber will peel and melt if heated. However, I don't advise you try this!

- A better test is to sniff the amber – warm it in your hands first. If it smells of pine tree resin, it's probably genuine.

- Saltwater test. Because amber has a low density, often helped by air bubbles, it is buoyant in seawater. For this test, add two to three tablespoons of salt to half a pint (or 250ml) of cold water. Drop in the piece of amber. True amber floats.

- Look for chips around bead holes

- Amber is warm to the touch

- Be suspicious if you see red amber! It's more likely to be re-constituted or bakelite, but can also be glass – which is much heavier.

- Copal is flaky, whereas amber is not. You can rub copal and bits will usually flake off (depending on its age).

Southwold Beach, Suffolk

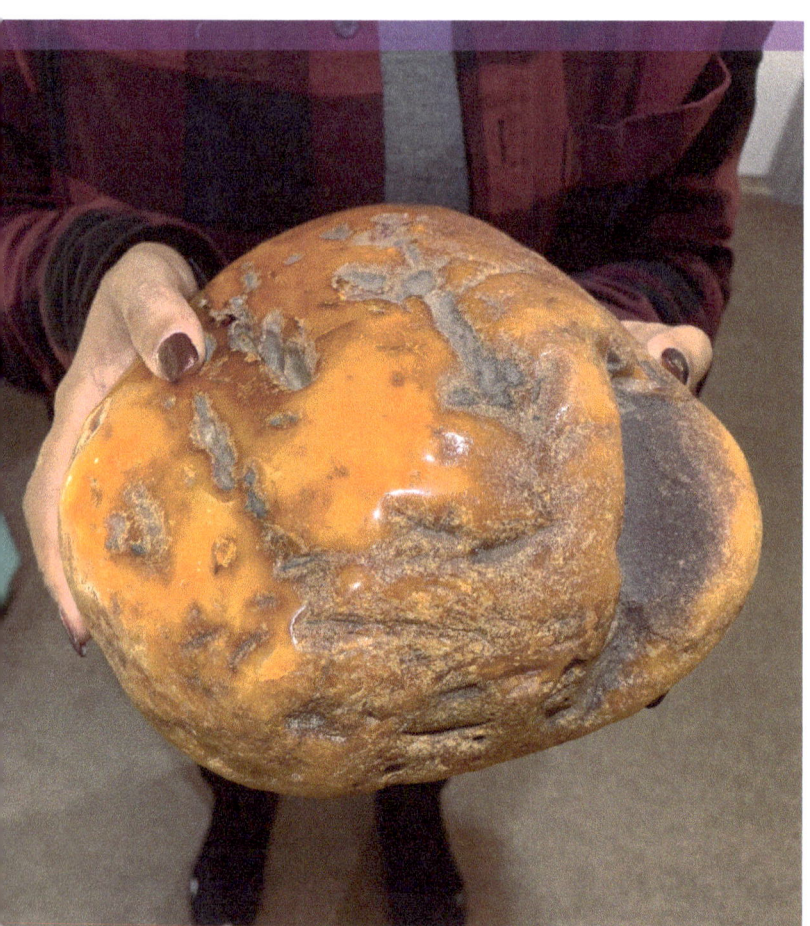

Largest piece of amber found in the UK. Brought up by a North Sea trawler in 2002 and weighs 2.2kg. Resides at the Amber Shop & Museum, Southwold.
© Kim Rix

Caring for amber
Wash in warm soapy water and polish with a clean soft cloth. For a deeper clean, use T-cut or Brasso and polish off with a clean cloth. Avoid contact with anything containing alcohol, such as perfumes, hairspray and detergent. Avoid excessive heat and light.

 Top Tip: Amber is soft and can be chipped with a knife or other hard objects.

The Amber Shop & Museum, Southwold © Kim Rix

About Blue John

Blue John, a variety of fluorite, is a soft gemstone that measures only 4 on the Mohs scale of hardness. It forms in bands of blue-purple and yellow-white on the walls and within the cavities of limestone caves. Intriguingly, we still don't know exactly what causes Blue John's blue colour as gemmologists have found none of the impurities that usually produce that shade. Most likely is that the colour arises from a disturbance in the arrangement of the stone's atoms – a phenomenon called **crystal lattice dislocation.**

The name Blue John is often believed to have derived from the French 'bleu-jaune' which means 'blue-yellow', though Blue John's range of colours also includes purple and white.

Gemstone quality Blue John is found in only two places in the UK and both are in the East Midlands English county of Derbyshire. It is said to have been mined in Derbyshire since Roman times, though there is no solid evidence that the Romans, who mined lead here, used it. Our earliest reference to the stone is in a letter dated 1766.

Buyer beware! A Blue John carving (left) and a Chinese carving (right)

BUYING GEMSTONES AND JEWELLERY

The famous industrialist Matthew Boulton's negotiations to lease the local Blue John mine suggest that the gemstone had been mined here for centuries.

The two Blue John mines, Treak Cliff Cavern and Blue John Cavern, lie in a remote valley within the Peak District. Both mines are still active, using a combination of traditional methods and new technologies to extract the fragile mineral from the rock without damaging it. Once at the surface, the pieces are examined and the best specimens are selected for jewellery and other ornaments. However, Blue John needs 18 months to dry out properly and hardened before its main treatment can begin; heating, binding with a mixture of resin and hardener, then more heating. After this process, Blue John is carefully cut into slices with each finished piece in mind.

A genuine Blue John carving

Blue John's heyday came during the Georgian period, when goblets, vases and other ornaments made of the gemstone became popular. At this point, miners were extracting up to 20 tonnes every year. Today, there are only 15 known seams of Blue John and it's uncertain how much of the gemstone still lies in the Derbyshire rock. In recent years, the mines have produced around half a tonne of Blue John per annum, which is the maximum allowed under mining restrictions designed to protect the supply. These restrictions, along with the uncovering of a forgotten seam in 2013 and the discovery of an entirely new vein in 2015, should see this level of production sustained for a reasonable length of time yet.

How to spot a fake
Fake Blue John usually has a plastic feel and sounds like plastic when tapped on another stone. Even if made of glass, it will tend to feel lightweight. A fake will often look too bright and too uniform – the colours in genuine fluorite tend to be muted and have less frequent or uniform colour banding. Price is also a good indicator, as Blue John is expensive.

How to care for Blue John
Blue John is a soft gemstone. Though treated with resin to make it more durable, it must be handled with care. Wrap it separately to store it and clean using only soap, water and a soft brush.

Where to find Blue John in the UK
The two remaining Blue John mines are popular tourist attractions, offering guided tours of the excavations and caves. Because they are relatively small enterprises, your guide might even be one of the miners or cutters themselves, giving you a great insight into the industry.

BUYING GEMSTONES AND JEWELLERY

Blue John Cavern
Visit: www.bluejohn-cavern.co.uk

Inside the Blue John Cavern, Castleton, Derbyshire © Kim Rix

Treak Cliff Cavern
Visit: www.bluejohnstone.com

Mining for Blue John. The Treak Cliff Cavern experience © Kim Rix

Kim's best find from Treak Cliff Cavern – Blue John fluorite © Kim Rix

BUYING GEMSTONES AND JEWELLERY

Recommended: The Blue John Experience at Treak Cliff Cavern – you'll be taken to the mining area to prospect for your own piece of Blue John stone.

Also worth a visit: If you're planning a trip to the Derbyshire mines, you shouldn't miss the opportunity to visit nearby Chatsworth House, the home of the Duke and Duchess of Devonshire. Chatsworth is one of England's largest and finest stately homes. Here you can see several Blue John ornaments and the stunning Blue John window commissioned by Georgiana Cavendish (the late 18th century Duchess of Devonshire, who was a keen mineral collector).
Visit: www.chatsworth.org

 Top Tip: While you're in Derbyshire, keep your eye out for Pietra Dura items made from Ashford black marble.

Ashford black marble inlaid with malachite, mother of pearl and colourful corals © Kim Rix

The beautiful landscape viewed from Castleton, in the High Peak district of Derbyshire © Kim Rix

BUYING GEMSTONES AND JEWELLERY

Other gemstones and minerals found in Great Britain

Though Great Britain is probably best known for its jet, amber and Blue John, you may well be tempted by the other beautiful gems on offer! A number of other interesting gemstones and minerals have been found across England, Scotland and Wales, including zircon, amethyst, pearl, topaz, tourmaline, turquoise and serpentine.

This chapter gives you a brief guide to the other gems you're most likely to find in Great Britain.

Scottish agate

Scotland has a great variety of agates. This gemstone is formed in volcanic rocks in central and western Scotland and has a long history – examples of worked agates from Neolithic times have been unearthed. The most famous site for Scottish agates is the Blue Hole near Montrose, whose deep blue and white agates were particularly popular in the 19th century.

Agate is a translucent, banded form of chalcedony and silica that comes in a wide range of colours. The colours occur in bands caused by differing impurities as the layers formed within the stone. The best quality agate is used in jewellery.

The best way to find agate is by beachcombing. For every thousand stones, you might find one agate. You have to put in the time and the miles! Note that most posters and images show semi-precious agate after it has been sliced but this is not how you'll find them among the pebbles and sand unless they've had some catastrophic break – which is highly unlikely given their hardness! Agates found on the beach normally come tumbled and weathered out. You might find some good agates on Lunan Bay.

BUYING GEMSTONES AND JEWELLERY

In Scotland, you will find the best places for beachcombing are: Tentsmuir, Elephant Rock, Boddin Point (100% pebble beach), Inverbervie Beach (all stones and pebbles), Tangeleha Beach, Scurdie Ness (Ferryden) beyond the lighthouse at Montrose and the Isle of Mull (West Coast).

Elephant Rock, Montrose © Kim Rix

Directions to Elephant Rock: From Boddin, go back to the road and walk along the footpath behind the white house. Follow the coastal park for about ten minutes. It's good for agates but take care – it's a very steep climb down. There is a small pebble area at the foot of the elephant.

There is not much parking at Boddin Point. Take care parking on the road.

There is car parking at Tangeleha Beach (Montrose) on a single track road.

Lunan Bay is a beautiful sandy beach with a free public gated car park (capacity 100 vehicles) operated by Angus Council – at the very end of a single track road. There is a river mouth with pebbles.

Some of Paul Moreland's private collection of agates © Kim Rix

BUYING GEMSTONES AND JEWELLERY

Agate found in Scurdie Ness (Ferryden) © Kim Rix

Agate found on Inverbervie Beach © Kim Rix

Tips for agate hunting:

- Follow the tide out. Light rain is perfect weather for agate hunting – just enough to make the stones shine.

- You can go one day and find nothing. Go back the following day and the action of the waves might have exposed the agate. Never give up!

- Look for agates close to the water's edge, where they are still wet. Look for colour.

- The best time to go looking for agates on the beach is during the winter, especially after a storm. The sea conditions are a lot rougher, so more stones get washed in.

- Whilst looking for agates, keep an eye out for jaspers.

- If you find stones that sparkle – that's iron pyrite, also known as fool's gold!

Caring for agate: Wash with warm, soapy water.

How to spot fake agate: Glass 'agate' may contain bubbles and obvious swirls of colour rather than bands. It's hard to imitate the natural banding of agate. Very brightly coloured agate is probably dyed.

Also worth a visit: Montrose Museum and Art Gallery. Look out for the collection of Scottish agates from the Panmure Collection.

Amethyst

A type of quartz, Scottish amethyst is found in many locations but especially Dumfries and Galloway. For the Scots the colour has a particular meaning, as it's similar to that of their national flower, the thistle. Jewellers have made the most of this association, using amethyst to represent the flower.

Caring for amethyst: wash in warm, soapy water

How to spot fake amethyst: Real amethyst feels cool to the touch and takes a few seconds to warm up when placed on the skin. Glass warms much faster and may contain bubbles or streaks/patches of dye.

Scottish amethyst – Treasures of the Earth Museum © Kim Rix

Fluorite

Fluorite (fluorspar) is found in several countries worldwide and has a range of uses in industry. First discovered by the Romans as a by-product of lead mining, fluorite was originally named 'murrina' and used as a decorative material. A fine example is the Crawford Cup, which dates from the 1st-2nd centuries AD and is on display at the British Museum. It wasn't until the 16th century that German scientist Georgius Agricola discovered that it could be used as a flux for smelting metals – hence the name fluorite, which derives from the Latin word 'fluere', 'to flow'.

Fluorite occurs in many colours, including duck egg blue, yellow, red, purple and green (as well as colourless) and in its cubic crystal form is highly collectable. Blue John, with its pretty hues, was popular with the Victorians, who used it for decorative items, brooches, perfume bottles, bell pulls, etc, together with urns, tassas (a shallow bowl with a stem), candlesticks and eggs. Miners would collect cubes of fluorite, which they named the '**bonny bits**' and used to create decorative displays called 'spar boxes'. You can see some exquisite examples in Killhope Museum's collection in County Durham. The museum also has an excellent display of fluorite specimens from the mines in the area.

Spar Box – bonny bits © Kim Rix

Visit: www.killhope.org.uk

Weardale Fluorite indoors (top) and outdoors (bottom) © Kim Rix

Fluorite gave its name to the phenomenon of fluorescence – when a substance absorbs electromagnetic radiation and emits it back as visible light. In Britain, only fluorite from the mines around Weardale in County Durham and Allenheads in Northumberland has fluorescence. Blue John does not fluoresce.

Weardale is famous for its fluorite, but the area is now a protected geopark and collecting is very difficult. Nothing significant remains on the surface, though if you walk around the old mines you might just spot the odd fragment glistening among the dirt and stones.

Worth a visit: The Weardale Show: a small show, normally held in August, following in the traditions of the early local shows that were an opportunity for everyone to see mineral treasures from the area.

How to care for fluorite: Fluorite is very soft – it chips and scratches very easily. Make sure you wrap it before storing with other jewellery. Fluorite can be cleaned with tepid water and a mild soap.

BUYING GEMSTONES AND JEWELLERY

 Top Tip: contrary to what you might find on Google, fluorite cannot be confused with halite. Halite is a very soft mineral which will dissolve in water and in damp conditions. Fluorite usually has a shiny lustre, whereas halite does not.

Garnet

'Garnet' is an umbrella term for a group of closely related varieties of mineral. The six main species are pyrope, almandine, spessartine, grossular, uvarovite and andradite, but within these species are several different varieties, too!

Garnets occur in a range of colours, but Scottish ones are orange and purple-red. Colour is the main factor affecting a garnet's value, with vivid red and brilliant green being the most coveted. Warm reddish hessonite (a variety of grossular) is the most commonly-occurring garnet, and the orange-coloured spessartine the most expensive.

Elie garnet found in Ruby Bay, Fife
© Kim Rix

Though garnets tend to be clean stones on the whole, some types such as spessartine and hessonite have been known to contain inclusions (flaws). Sometimes these flaws can produce a light effect called **asterism** – making a star shape appear to float across the gemstone's surface. Star garnets are rare to find.

Garnet has been used in jewellery for thousands of years and was a favourite of civilisations dating as far back as the Bronze Age. It's rare to find a gem-studded piece of Anglo-Saxon jewellery that doesn't use garnets and, during the Crusades, garnet was used as a protective talisman against the enemy.

Caring for garnet: Garnet is not a hard stone. Measuring 6.5-7.5 on the Mohs scale, it's prone to scratching and therefore is not ideal in rings worn every day. Do not steam clean garnets. You may put your garnet in an ultrasonic cleaner, except for demantoid garnet. If in doubt, clean your garnet with warm soapy water and a soft brush.

How to spot a fake: The easiest method is to look at the garnet in both natural and artificial light. Take it outdoors, then bring it indoors. Does the colour look slightly different in each light? A real garnet should look a slightly different colour as conditions vary. Look through the stone – if you see lots of inclusions, your stone is probably not a garnet. Garnets generally have good clarity.

Where to find Scottish garnets: Elie Bay, on the East Coast between Edinburgh and St Andrews, is also known as 'Ruby Bay' thanks to the garnets nestling in the shingle on its beach. You can also try Glen Esk (up in the hills where the river runs into Montrose).

 Top tip: You'll need to put in the hours if you want to find yourself some Scottish garnets. Head for the shingle and look out for the gems glinting in the sun.

Jasper

Jasper is a variety of quartz. Scottish Jasper is mostly found in the Campsie Fells, a range of volcanic hills north of Glasgow. You can also find it in the Scottish Borders, north of the Cheviot Hills. Here, the high iron content makes the jasper red or yellow. Queen Victoria popularised it and 'Scottish pebble jewellery' became very fashionable in the 19th century.

Note that you'll need a good level of fitness to climb the Campsie Fells! The highest point, Earl's Seat, rises to 578m. I'd advise you not to go alone – join a field trip instead.

Scottish Jasper © *Two Skies, Scotland*

Scottish sapphire

Sapphire is a variety of the mineral corundum and occurs in many different colours (though not red – red corundum is always known as ruby). Measuring 9 on the Mohs scale, it's one of the hardest gemstones apart from diamond. Scottish sapphires tend to be small and not of the quality you'd expect to find in places like south-east Asia, but their rarity makes them valuable and highly desirable.

Around the corner from Luskentyre beach, Isle of Harris © Kim Rix

There are a number of sapphire locations in Scotland, all of which are protected as SSSI and thus difficult for the general public to explore. The part of Scotland most famous for sapphires is the Isle of Harris. Harris is part of the Outer Hebrides, a remote group of islands off the very north-west coast of Scotland. Back in the 1980s, several small, light blue sapphires were found during the construction of a farm path and a huge (though heavily fractured) 242-carat sapphire was unearthed in 1995. Though an exciting discovery for the island, this led to 'collectors' and commercial interests visiting the site and stripping it of any material of worth. Subsequently the area was designated an SSSI, though an anomaly in the legislation that protects it allows the collecting of loose material. However, Scottish Natural Heritage and the landowner understandably do not welcome people visiting!

Scottish pearl

Pearl is formed when a small piece of grit or shell becomes lodged within the body of a mollusc such as an oyster or mussel. To protect its soft body, the mollusc secretes a mucus which hardens to form a coating around the object. Scottish pearls are produced by a fascinating freshwater mussel *(Margaritifera margaritifera)* that grows to 140mm in length and can live to 100 years old.

Unfortunately, heavy fishing of Scottish pearl mussels since pre-Roman times has driven them almost to extinction and Scottish pearls are now subject to draconian legislation. In 1998, the Scottish pearl mussel was awarded full protection status, making it an offence to kill, injure, take, intentionally disturb or damage their habitat. Dealers may legally sell jewellery using pearls collected before 1998, but only once granted a governmental licence. Naturally, this makes Scottish pearl jewellery rather expensive!

Top Tip: Do not expect to be able to buy loose, unmounted pearls – only those that have already been set in jewellery.

If you're tempted to buy, Scottish pearls come in several shades, including white, cream, pinkish orange, grey, brown and lilac. When you buy Scottish pearls, your jewellery will come with a licence number from Scottish Natural Heritage, as well as buyer documentation. Make sure you keep this documentation, as it is proof of legal provenance if you ever need to resell or claim on insurance.

Those who are content with merely looking can see some beautiful Scottish freshwater pearls adorning the Scottish crown and royal sceptre, on display at Edinburgh Castle.

A string of Scottish pearls © Alistir Tate

Know the law:
- Fishing for Scottish river pearls is illegal!

- It is illegal to possess freshwater pearl mussels or pearls collected since 1998, when the law was changed to give the species further protection.

- It is illegal to sell, or advertise for sale, Scottish freshwater pearl mussels or their pearls, unless under licence from NatureScot, the Scottish agency for nature.

Caring for pearls: It is important to store pearls in silk or chamois leather when not in use, away from other gemstones and metal to avoid scratching. They should lie flat, to avoid the thread stretching. To clean them, wipe gently after use to remove traces of perspiration or perfume.

How to spot a fake: generally speaking, the surface of an authentic natural pearl is gritty and its shape uneven. It will also feel cold to the touch. Imitation pearls, on the other hand, will feel warm, look beautifully smooth and be perfectly rounded. Look around the hole to detect chipped paint and through the hole to detect glass or plastic.

Serpentine

Serpentine doesn't refer to one particular gem, but rather a group of related minerals. Usually green, serpentine's name is thought to derive from its resemblance to the skin of a snake. The best places to look for it in Britain are Portsoy in the north-east of Scotland and The Lizard peninsula in Cornwall.

Portsoy marble

Portsoy marble is a type of serpentine found in Portsoy on the north-east coast of Scotland. This particular variety – bowenite to be precise – is an especially beautiful red and green that entranced Louis XIV, who had pillars of Portsoy marble installed in the Palace of Versailles. The town is justifiably proud of its gemstone and many of the houses in Portsoy are inlaid with it.

Serpentine stone is quite soft and easily damaged. As the natural stone is very porous, it's likely that any cut and polished stone you buy will have been treated with a protective penetrating sealer.

Portsoy's quarry has been closed since the late 1700s, but you can still find serpentine pebbles on the beach, where the quarry spoils

Portsoy Harbour in Aberdeenshire © *Kim Rix*

were emptied. Climb down the brae to the beach when the tide is right out and look where the waves and rain have made the pebbles wet and brought out the colour, making the serpentine easier to spot. It can be tricky to recognise it, until washed and polished. It has also become quite rare, so if you don't find any on the beach, you can always try the harbourside shops in Portsoy.

Other marble found in Scotland: Highland marble, Skye marble, Iona marble

Skye marble - photo taken at the Treasure Hut, Isle of Skye © Kim Rix

Cornish serpentine (Lizardite)

Cornish serpentine, found on The Lizard peninsula therefore also known as lizardite, is said to be the finest serpentine in the world. Made popular by Prince Albert in the 19th century, Lizard's serpentine was in great demand during the Victorian age. Nowadays, only a few local craftspeople remain. The colours in Cornish serpentine form a striking blend of red, green and grey.

Local legend tells that serpentine was discovered here by a shipwrecked sailor, who noticed how cattle had rubbed against and thus polished a serpentine rock. However it's more likely that locals using cobbles and flagstones made from serpentine noticed the stone's beauty, as daily footfall began to polish the rock.

Portsoy marble © *Kim Rix*

How to care for serpentine: Serpentine is rather soft and fragile. Use only a soft cloth and warm water to clean serpentine gemstones. To avoid scratching, store away from other jewellery.

 Top tip: Be aware that serpentine is often falsely sold as nephrite jade.

Tourmaline

Roche Rock, near St Austell in Cornwall, is a geological site of interest with a unique outcrop of tourmaline.

Tourmaline gets its name from a Sinhalese phrase 'tura mali', which means 'stone mixed with many colours'. The presence of different elements in tourmaline's makeup produces its plethora of colour variations. Many tourmalines have more than one colour within the same stone. Watermelon tourmaline, with its layers of pink and green, is the best known of these varieties. Some tourmalines seem to change colour under different light sources and some display chatoyancy, which gives them the appearance of a cat's eye.

You won't find such colourful specimens at Roche Rock, but the rocky outcrops are a fascinating example of quartz shorl – tourmalinised granite, with black tourmaline crystals.

Tourmaline has some interesting properties. Famous 19th century art critic and polymath John Ruskin once described the chemical makeup of tourmaline as being 'more like a doctor's prescription than the making of a reputable mineral'! Swedish botanist Carl Von Linne described tourmaline as 'the electric' stone because it acquires an electrical charge when rubbed, attracting small particles like dust.

How to care for tourmaline: Tourmaline jewellery is best cleaned with warm water and a soft cloth. To minimise scratching, keep your tourmaline away from other jewellery.

Roche Rock tourmaline

Quartz

If you're hunting for a souvenir of Scotland, you can't go wrong with Scottish quartz – the national gemstone of Scotland.

Scottish quartz is most famously associated with the Cairngorm mountains, site of Balmoral, home to Queen Victoria and her successors. This is where the famous '**Cairngorm quartz**' is found, in colours of smoky amber, grey and, occasionally, black. A great gemstone for patriots, Scottish quartz is often used to adorn traditional highland dress.

Cairngorm quartz crystal
© Two Skies, Scotland

Another variety of British quartz is known as Buxton diamond. Buxton quartz was locally referred to as Buxton or Derbyshire diamond and early published papers suggest that it used to be relatively abundant. Though it's not a particularly convincing diamond simulant, Buxton quartz crystals can be highly attractive in their own right and are now highly sought after due to their rarity.

Quartz has also been found in Snowdonia, Wales, and in Cornwall – at St Nectan's Glen (Tintagel) as well as inland in the old silver, gold and tin mines.

Quartz with chlorite, Tintagel
© John Burrows – Albion Fire and Ice

BUYING GEMSTONES AND JEWELLERY

Welsh gold

Buying Welsh gold can be tricky and, as with buying gemstones, the genuine article has considerable value whilst imitations have a lot less. There is so much false and inaccurate information being shared I urge you not to believe everything you hear or read, especially on the internet.

Here are some genuine facts about Welsh gold:

- Welsh gold is considered to be the rarest in the world.

- Welsh gold has decorated the ring finger of every royal bride since the Queen Mother's wedding in 1923. It's true – the Crown has its own supply!

- The history of Welsh gold adornments goes all the way back to the Bronze Age. Visitors to the British Museum can view the 3000-year-old 'Mold Cape', an intricately fashioned object made from a large quantity of gold that in all likelihood was mined in Wales.

- The Romans also mined gold during their occupation of South Wales, leaving behind many coins and pieces of Welsh gold jewellery upon abandoning Britain.

- Welsh gold is often regarded as having a rosier colour than other gold, but that's a myth. The rosy

Welsh gold – my retirement fund sorted! © Kim Rix

colour is due to traces of copper in the alloy – if separated from the copper traces, it would be as yellow as gold from any other source. This myth dates back to the Victorian era, when there were numerous active mining operations in Wales and the Victorians liked to use copper in their gold alloys.

- Two major seams of Welsh gold were rediscovered during the industrial revolution: one in the north and one in the south of the country. At its height, the gold mining industry in Wales produced nearly 20,000 ounces of gold per year (worth about £25mn in today's terms).

- Mining in Great Britain ceased to be commercially viable some decades ago. With no new gold being mined, the price of Welsh gold has rocketed and can attract bids at auction of up to 30 times the value of standard gold.

- Ever wondered why some gold rings turn your fingers green? A gold alloy can qualify for a 9k assay stamp even if it's just 37% gold. So what else is in there? A good quality alloy will be gold, silver and just a trace of copper. (The more copper, the rosier the colour.) Poor quality alloys can have a high nickel or tin content and it is these that can discolour your fingers.

Hallmarks

When buying Welsh gold jewellery, check the hallmark. Forgeries are widespread.

Issued by the assay office, a hallmark essentially guarantees the quality and make-up of the alloy, together with the maker's mark. There are also optional additional marks which anyone can put on an item.

BUYING GEMSTONES AND JEWELLERY

There are five key elements to a traditional British hallmark and a genuine one should tell you where it was hallmarked, what it is made of, when it was created and who created it.

The five marks comprise:

> Assay Office town mark – where
> Metal Fineness marks (two marks) – what
> Date letter – when
> A Sponsor's mark (also known as the Maker's mark) – who

Gwern Gwynfil, from the Welsh Gold Center in Tragaron, says: 'Maker's Marks have to be made public but for the handful of pure Welsh Gold items we make, we have created a stamp which ensures provenance and this will only be published when it is destroyed – to limit the chances of anyone copying it – especially whilst it can still be matched to a date stamp. It is the combination of stamps, design and origin together, which create very strong provenance.'

Welsh gold nuggets on a traditional Welsh woollen blanket – Melin Teifi design
© Kim Rix

Where to visit:

Dolaucothi Gold Mine: Near Llanwrda, south-west Wales.
The Dolaucothi Gold Mine is the only known Roman gold mine in the UK, although experts suspect that other, as yet undiscovered, archaeological sites exist.

The mine was still in regular use right up until 1938 and the area was left to the National Trust in 1941, who turned it into an archaeological site and tourist attraction. Visitors can go on a guided tour and learn how to pan for gold.

River Cothi: Head down to the nearby River Cothi, where you may just be lucky enough to spot the odd speck of gold gleaming in the gravel. But do be aware that it is an SSSI.

Dolaucothi Gold Mine © *Kim Rix*

Need to know:

- First and foremost, provenance is the key to value in Welsh gold jewellery!

- Ask the question "How much Welsh gold is there in it?" 5% is good. 10% is much better. However 'a touch of Welsh gold' could mean virtually none!

- Beware of people selling rose gold as Welsh gold.

- Pure gold (24k, 99.95% purity) is of little use in jewellery, as it is rather soft. Gold is therefore usually alloyed with other metals, to increase the strength. The gold karat weight increases with the percentage of gold.

- Test it. Gold, silver and platinum are **not magnetic**.

- Some jewellers do still make pure Welsh gold items, but they are indeed very expensive.

- Polish it. Rub the gold on a cloth. Real gold will leave no mark, while gold plate will leave gold-coloured residue on the cloth.

- It's important not to confuse the Clogau brand of jewellery (manufactured in the Far East) with the goldmine known as Clogau St David's – they are not the same.

Scottish gold

Scotland's only commerical gold mine is located in the Loch Lomond and Trossachs National Park. Scotgold Resources started extracting commercial quantities of gold there in 2020 and have named the mine 'Cononish', which is Gaelic for 'where the waters meet'. Currently only two jewellers in Great Britain are licensed to make and sell Scottish gold jewellery from the Cononish mine:

www.sheilafleet.com and www.hamiltonandinches.com.

Hoping to catch a glimpse of Nessy! © Kim Rix

Gold panning

Need to know: The Law
Permission

Before panning anywhere, you need to make sure you have the permission of the landowner. It's best to get this in writing – noting that the owner of the riverbank and the owner of the surrounding farmland might not be the same person! It's the owner of the riverbank whose permission you need. Not only that, but the mineral rights to the area might belong to someone completely different. Do your homework!

Anyone planning to search for gold or silver by any method should be aware that, in almost all cases, gold and silver is considered property of The Crown. The Crown Estate does not license the removal of gold by panning because of its potential environmental impact.
As a side note, Scottish gold isn't as highly regulated as Scottish pearls and laws are rarely enforced in relation to recreational and hobby panning, but they are worth bearing in mind.

Popular areas for panning in Great Britain

England
Most British gold is found in Wales or Scotland.
- Nenthead (northern Pennines)
- River Swale
- Cambourne
- Falmouth

Scotland
- The Lowther Hills around Wanlockhead. The Lowther and Buccleuch Estates issue gold panning licences for the area.
- The Leadhills, Wanlockhead. A protected area for geology and wildlife. You can find maps which set out the extent of the SSSI at https://sitelink.nature.scot/site/915

- The Suisgill Estate in northern Scotland
  Visit: www.suisgill.co.uk/things-to-do/gold-panning
  Recreational gold panning is permitted free of charge in two rivers on the estate, but strict guidelines apply.
- The Kildonan area near Helmsdale, on the east coast of Sutherland.
- Aberfeldy – people pan in the rivers around Aviemore.

Gold and gem panning with Highland Safaris, Aberfeldy © *Kim Rix*

Wales
- Snowdonia National Park, particularly the Afon Wen and Afon Mawddach ('afon' is Welsh for 'river').
- River Cothi in Camarthenshire, location of the Dolaucothi Gold Mine.
- Llanfrynach in Pembrokeshire.
- Parys Mountain, Anglesey.

BUYING GEMSTONES AND JEWELLERY

Museums with gemstone and mineral collections

England

The Crown Jewels, London

The Coronation Regalia, to give the Crown Jewels their official name, have been kept in the Tower of London since the 17th century. They are one of Great Britain's most popular tourist attractions, with around 3 million visitors per year.

Don't miss Cullinan I, the world's largest top-quality cut diamond at 530.2 carats, or the Imperial State Crown, which the monarch wears at the opening of parliament. The Imperial State Crown contains a staggering 2868 diamonds, 17 sapphires, 11 emeralds, 269 pearls and 4 rubies, though the famous 'Black Prince's Ruby' is actually a spinel.

Visit: www.hrp.org.uk/tower-of-london/whats-on/the-crown-jewels

The Victoria and Albert Museum, London

The V&A is home to a jewellery collection of over 6000 pieces, making it one of the biggest collections in the world. The collection holds pieces that span the millennia, from Ancient Egypt to the present day. You can see jewellery given by Queen Elizabeth I to her courtiers, diamonds worn by Catherine the Great of Russia and an emerald necklace given by Napoleon to his adopted daughter.

Visit: www.vam.ac.uk/collections/jewellery#intro

Natural History Museum, London

The museum's collection houses a mind-blowing 500,000 specimens, which researchers can search online. A wonderful selection of these is displayed in original Victorian oak display cabinets in the museum's vast mineralogy hall, including samples of Hope's Nose gold from Devon and the largest blue topaz gemstone found. Make your way to The Vault to see some of nature's most unique and valuable treasures, as well as the world's largest collection of coloured diamonds.

Visit: www.nhm.ac.uk/our-science/collections/mineralogy-collections.html

Wollaton Hall, Nottingham
Wollaton Hall is a splendid Grade 1 listed Elizabethan building that houses Nottingham's Natural History Museum. Its collection includes over 5000 specimens.

Visit: www.wollatonhall.org.uk

Oxford University Museum of Natural History, Oxford
Oxford's Museum of Natural History has a fine collection of gemstones, including natural crystals, faceted stones and carvings of all the well-known gems, as well as the more unusual types.

Visit: www.oumnh.ox.ac.uk

The Buxton Museum, Bishop Auckland
The Buxton Museum has a fine collection of minerals, including Blue John and other local specimens. You will find some impressive examples of worked Blue John and local marble in the art gallery.

Visit: www.derbyshire.gov.uk/leisure/buxton-museum

Museum of Whitby Jet
Visit: www.museumofwhitbyjet.com

BUYING GEMSTONES AND JEWELLERY

The Amber Shop & Museum, Southwold
This small, interesting museum aims to educate visitors on the beauty and wonder of amber, particularly Baltic amber.

Visit: www.ambershop.co.uk

Royal Institution of Cornwall Museum, Truro
This fascinating museum has an internationally important collection of minerals, including some specimens (fluorite, for example) which are the finest in the world for their species. Give yourself an hour or three to explore the museum in its entirety, or just head straight to the mineral section.

Visit: www.royalcornwallmuseum.org.uk

Royal Institution of Cornwall Museum, Truro © Kim Rix

Ebor Jetworks Museum, Whitby

The Ebor Jetworks Museum is owned and run by Sarah Steele, one of Britain's leading jet experts. Though it's a small museum, you could easily spend an hour or two there, absorbing everything there is to know about jet, its history and heritage – and its many simulants.

Visit: www.eborjetworks.co.uk

Ebor Jetworks, Whitby © *Kim Rix*

Kim Rix holding one of Whitby's largest specimens of jet – with Sarah Steel at Ebor Jetworks © *Kim Rix*

BUYING GEMSTONES AND JEWELLERY

The Victorian Jetworks, Whitby

The Whitby Jet Heritage Centre is the only surviving Victorian workshop. It's been immaculately preserved. Meet 'The jet carver's daughter', Imogen, who will take you back through time to explain jet's jewellery making history.

Visit: www.whitbyjet.co.uk/victorian-workshop

The Victorian Jetworks, Whitby
© Kim Rix

The only surviving Victorian workshop, Whitby © Kim Rix

Crystal Classics Showroom, East Coker

Diana and Ian Bruce, directors of UK Mining Ventures, have together built up a spectacular collection of gemstones from all over the world. Showroom viewings by appointment.

Visit: www.crystalclassics.co.uk

Crystal Classics Showroom, East Coker © Kim Rix

Scotland

Montrose Museum and Art Gallery

The Montrose Museum and Art Gallery was one of the first purpose-built museums in Scotland and is home to an impressive collection of rocks, minerals and fossils.

Visit: www.angusalive.scot/museums-galleries/visit-a-museum-gallery/montrose-museum/

National Museum of Scotland

The National Museum of Scotland is based in Edinburgh and has over 2000 different mineral species in its Earth Sciences collection. Many of these can be seen online via the 'Museum at Home' section.

Visit: www.nms.ac.uk/national-museum-of-scotland

Hunterian Museum at the University of Glasgow

The Hunterian Museum has over 120,000 rock and mineral specimens in its collections, as well as around 1500 cut gemstones and 70 meteorites. Within this large geology collection, you can see Scottish Cairngorm quartz.

Visit: www.gla.ac.uk/hunterian

Gem Rock Museum and Crystal Cave, Creetown

This museum contains a fascinating collection of gemstones, crystals and minerals from Britain and around the world. The collection includes the 'Maverick' gold nugget, one of the largest natural gold specimens on display in Britain. Children will enjoy the Crystal Cave, created to show off the minerals in a realistic cave setting and including a display of mineral fluorescence.

Visit: www.gemrock.net

A collection of fluorescent minerals © Kim Rix

Treasures of the Earth Museum, Fort William

Housed in what was once a Catholic church, this museum displays an extensive private collection of crystals, gemstones and fossils, presented in an entertaining and educational way that appeals to children and adults alike. Allow 2 hours to explore.

Visit: www.treasuresoftheearth.co.uk

Kelvingrove, Glasgow

Glasgow's flagship museum had a major re-jig a few years ago and its collection of gemstones and minerals has been integrated into displays on Scotland's natural history. It's a good way to learn about rocks and minerals in context.

Cairngorm quartz display at Treasures of the Earth Museum © Kim Rix

Visit: www.glasgowlife.org.uk/museums/venues/kelvingrove-art-gallery-and-museum

Wales

The Welsh Gold Centre, Tregaron

It might be off the beaten track in a quiet town, but this place is much more than a museum and it's well worth spending a precious hour

BUYING GEMSTONES AND JEWELLERY

The Welsh Gold Centre, Tregaron © *Kim Rix*

or three here. Within the Welsh Gold Centre, there's a craft centre, art gallery, museum and café.

Visit: www.rhiannon.co.uk

National Museum of Wales, Cardiff

Wales's National Museum has over 40,000 mineral specimens in its collection, including the most complete suite of Welsh minerals. Supergene, hydrothermal, meteorite, igneous, metamorphic and sedimentary minerals – there's definitely something here to amaze everyone. Leave lots of time to explore the rest of the museum, too.

Visit: www.museum.wales/cardiff

The iconic Cuillins, a range of rocky mountains located on the Isle of Skye in Scotland © Kim Rix

BUYING GEMSTONES AND JEWELLERY

Famous British treasure hoards

The Staffordshire Hoard, Birmingham and Stoke-on-Trent

The Staffordshire Hoard was discovered in 2009 and consists of over 3500 gold and silver military artefacts from around the 5th or 6th century AD. It is the largest collection of Anglo-Saxon gold ever found. Many of the pieces are inlaid with garnets from as far away as Sri Lanka and Afghanistan.

Cheek Piece, Staffordshire Hoard

Items from the Staffordshire Hoard are on display at the Birmingham Museum & Art Gallery and The Potteries Museum and Art Gallery.

Visit: www.staffordshirehoard.org.uk

Cheapside Hoard, London

The Cheapside Hoard was discovered by workmen in 1912. Lying beneath a City of London cellar was an enormous cache of Elizabethan and Stuart treasure, hidden there some 300 years previously. The hoard consists of nearly 500 gemstone and jewellery items, reflecting the hoard's location – Cheapside was once the goldsmith's quarter and London's main shopping street. The hoard was probably the stock in trade of a goldsmith. At the time of writing this book, the hoard was not yet on display – it's awaiting a permanent, purpose-built home in a new museum, due to open in 2024.

Tourist attractions

Sadly, other than beachcombing, legislation means that there are few places in Great Britain that a tourist can 'have a go' at digging for crystals and minerals. This is best done with a club-organised field trip. However, there are a few places where you can get closer to the action and have a hands-on experience.

The Museum Of Lead Mining, Wanlockhead, England
At the Wanlockhead Museum of Lead Mining, you'll be able to take a course on gold panning and enjoy the visitor centre's display of minerals, gold and other local artefacts.

Visit: www.leadminingmuseum.co.uk

Killhope Lead Mining Museum, Bishop Auckland, England
The Killhope Museum immerses visitors in mining history, with mine tours and a museum among many activities on offer. The mineral gallery has a magnificent selection of minerals commonly found in the North Pennines.

Visit: www.killhope.org.uk

Highland Safaris, Aberfeldy
They offer a range of exciting outdoor activities including a gold and gem panning experience.

Visit: www.highlandsafaris.net

National Stone Centre, Wirksworth near Matlock Bath, Derbyshire
The National Stone Centre educates visitors about geology and offers gem panning as one of the activities at its discovery centre.

Visit: www.nationalstonecentre.org.uk

BUYING GEMSTONES AND JEWELLERY IN **GREAT BRITAIN**

Dolaucothi Gold Mine, Pumsaint, near Llanwrda, Wales
At Dolaucothi, you can take a trip into the old Victorian and early 20th century workings, view the remains of the Roman gold mines and have a go at gold panning. The mines are owned and run by The National Trust.

Visit: www.nationaltrust.org.uk/dolaucothi-gold-mines

Cornwall Gold and Tolgus Mill, Redruth, Cornwall
Tolgus Mill gives visitors an education on tin mining and smelting. In the workshop, you can see local jewellers create Cornish jewellery from tin ore recovered from the stream running through the site.

Visit: www.cornwall-gold.com

Tipping mine tubs, Treasures of the Earth © Kim Rix

BUYING GEMSTONES AND JEWELLERY

How to become a gemstone collector

A private collection of gems and minerals collected in the UK © Kim Rix

Be nosy – be curious

If you're a nosy person, you're off to a good start. Be curious. Ask lots of questions. Use the internet to look for local gemmological and mineralogical societies and don't be scared to approach experts. Most will be thrilled that you share their love of gemstones and will be all too pleased to talk to you.

Buy some stones!

You need some gemstones for a gemstone collection, after all! Your starter stones don't need to be expensive or rare. Many stones can be found for very little cash in museum gift shops or new age stores, for example. Maybe you'd like specimens or perhaps you'd prefer to make your collection wearable by buying your stones already set in jewellery. You may find yourself drawn to particular stones, maybe because you love the colour or pattern. This is your collection, so you do you!

Build your knowledge

There are some great books and websites on gemstones and minerals out there. The publisher Dorling Kindersley produces some affordable and informative books, lavishly illustrated with photographs. The GIA, where I studied, has a website packed with easy-to-read information and many images of exquisite gemstones.

Invest in some basic kit

Once you know what you're looking for, you'll want the equipment to do it. A 10x jeweller's loupe, tweezers and a small torch are essential for examining gemstones up close. Think about where and how to display your collection, to show it off while keeping it safe.

Check out your local area

Are you living in an area known for a particular gemstone? Why not go on a field trip and hunt for specimens? You might be lucky and spot some colour on the surface. Make sure you double check your local laws on gemstone fossicking before you head out, though!

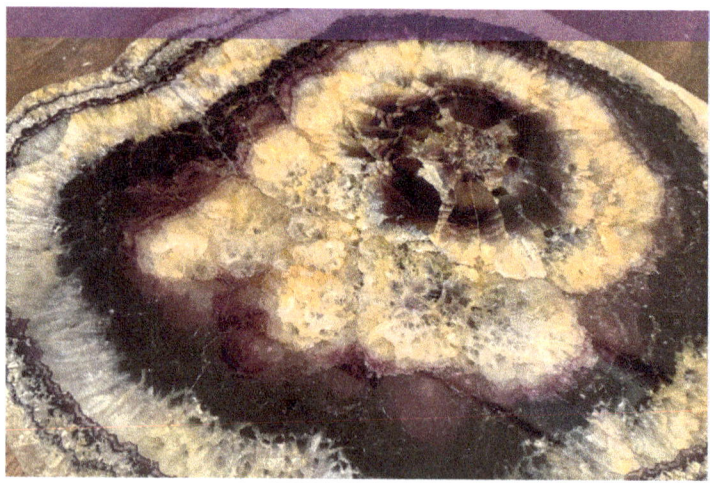

Cut from a stalagmite of Blue John © Kim Rix

BUYING GEMSTONES AND JEWELLERY

Rules and regulations of rock hunting

Those who started collecting in the 'rockhounding boom' of the 1960's and 1970's will know just how difficult it has become to go collecting these days. Today, you can go collecting yourself, but you must be aware of who owns the land – a farmer, the National Trust or the State – and then apply for permissions. It is quite likely that permission will be granted, but it might take weeks for this to happen. The advice from experts is to join a club.

Some areas have been designated as 'SSSI', which means that collecting there is now prohibited. If you ignore the rules, you risk prosecution as it is an offence to intentionally or recklessly damage the protected natural features of an SSSI, which includes removing natural objects from the area.

Boddin Point beach, Montrose © Kim Rix

Each area in England, Scotland and Wales has its own rules and regulations. The three countries have their own conservation bodies: Natural England , NatureScot and Natural Resources Wales. Though each has its own name and office, they all have the same aim of protecting sites of importance.

The onus is on the individual to check that what they are doing is legal. Natural England's website is updated regularly, so what might be legal today might be restricted in six months' time. It's really important to check beforehand!

Going through the Magic Map portal is the easiest way to negotiate your way. If a site is listed for the protection of one thing, then everything else within the site area is also protected. This last statement is true of course for protected sites in Great Britain.

Visit: www.magic.defra.gov.uk/MagicMap.aspx

Instructions
1. Click on the '+' symbol below the on-screen compass to zoom in on the detail.
2. Drag the map to your location using your mouse or touch screen.
3. Click on the 'i' identify tool in the toolbar at the top of the screen.
4. Using the crosshair, click on the map to find out the name of the SSSI.

The coastline is the place to go if you want to collect items that can be polished and turned into jewellery. However the National Trust is currently trying to buy more coastline via a project called Operation Neptune, especially in places like Cornwall. Over the years, they have acquired a lot of land and they are not too keen on people collecting.

BUYING GEMSTONES AND JEWELLERY

Lady Janet Anstruther's Tower, a man-made cave on Ruby Bay, Elie, Leven © Kim Rix

But they don't own the beaches. So long as you go below the high tide mark, no one is going to interfere – unless it's an SSSI, of course. You really must check that what you are doing is correct before you start.

The fines in England are horrendously high for those caught collecting for commercial purposes without permission. By and large, individual amateurs collecting for their own personal use are discouraged but not chased seriously.

Beachcombing top tips
- Always check the tide timings!
  Visit: www.bbc.co.uk/weather/coast-and-sea/tide-tables
- Do not collect close to the cliffs
- Never hammer into the cliffs
- Avoid shafts and depressions

Best times to go beachcombing
- When the tide is out
- During the tourist seasons, for safety (and the best weather, of course)
- After storms – they can wash interesting pieces onto the beach

Tools for beachcombing
- Good walking boots or wellies
- Gloves
- Small bags for your finds
- A rock hammer
- Other tools such as a rake, trowel or spade

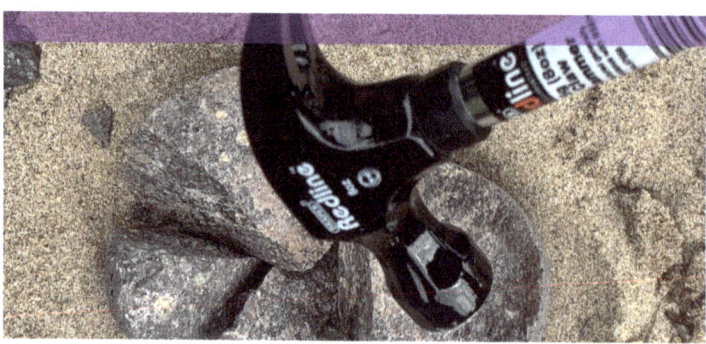

Take a good rock hammer when you go beachcombing © *Kim Rix*

Associations and Academies in Great Britain

If you are thinking about exploring a career in gemstones, here are a few routes to follow:

Gemmological Association of Great Britain (Gem-A)
Gem-A offers a range of short courses, workshops and lab classes.

Visit: www.gem-a.com

Gemological Institute of America (GIA)
The GIA has 10 locations around the world, including London, and offers a range of courses in person and online.

For London, visit: www.gia.edu/UK-EN/gem-education/london

Scottish Gemmological Association (SGA)
Formed in 2008, the SGA is closely affiliated with the Gemmological Association of Great Britain and promotes gemmology in Scotland.

Visit: www.scottishgemmology.org

Geologists' Association (GA)
Geology and gemmology are closely related subjects, so you can learn a lot about gemstones, their composition and formation from the Geologists' Association talks and publications.

Visit: www.geologistsassociation.org.uk

The Jewellers Academy for jewellery business courses and online jewellery making classes.

Visit: www.londonjewelleryschool.co.uk/pages/jewellers-academy

Clubs and societies

Gem and Mineral Clubs

Scottish Mineral and Lapidary Club
Visit: www.lapidary.org.uk

Sussex Mineral and Lapidary Society
Visit: www.smls.online

Collectors of British Minerals – a Facebook group, hosted by Matt Wall

UK Facet Cutters Guild (membership club)
Visit: www.ukfcg.org

The Russell Society (membership club) – named in honor of Sir Arthur Russell, the foremost British mineral collector of the 20th century. This society organises field trips.
Visit: www.russellsoc.org

Rockngem Magazine has a list of British clubs and associations as well as a list of all the mineral shows.
Visit: www.rockngem-magazine.co.uk

Gem and Mineral shows

Bakewell, Derbyshire
Visit: www.rockexchange.uk

Oxford shows – three times a year
Visit: www.10times.com/mineral-fossil-shows

Jewellery shows

Goldsmiths' Fair
Goldsmiths' Fair is a prestigious event that takes place annually at Goldsmiths' Hall in London and showcases some of the UK's finest contemporary jewellers.
Visit: www.goldsmithsfair.co.uk

London Craft Week
London Craft Week brings together makers from all over the world. Exhibitors include established brands and emerging talents.
Visit: www.londoncraftweek.com

The Jewellery Cut
Online platform The Jewellery Cut aims to elevate and celebrate the best of the UK's independent contemporary jewellery brands.
Visit: www.jewellerycut.com

Desire Jewellery Fairs
Desire Jewellery Fairs showcase a carefully curated group of contemporary jewellers, both established and emerging.
Visit: www.desirefair.com

Fair Luxury
Fair Luxury is an independent collective of jewellers working for sustainability and social justice in the jewellery industry.
Visit: www.fairluxury.co.uk

North East Open Studios (NEOS)
NEOS is a not-for-profit collective of artists, makers, and designers based in the north-east of Scotland. They hold a 9-day Open Studios event each September.
Visit: www.northeastopenstudios.co.uk

BUYING GEMSTONES AND JEWELLERY IN **GREAT BRITAIN**

How to find a jeweller

The National Association of Jewellers (NAJ) is the leading body for the UK's jewellery industry. It was formed in 2015 by merging the British Jewellers' Association (BJA) and the National Association of Goldsmiths (NAG). Its members are required to adhere to a strict code of conduct. You can search for a jeweller via the NAJ website.

Visit: www.naj.co.uk

How to find a jewellery valuer

The Jewellery Valuers Association is the only independent group in the UK specifically for professional jewellery and watch valuers, including specialists in various fields.

Visit: www.thejva.org/find-valuer

The Institute of Registered Valuers (IRV) is part of the National Association of Jewellers. You can search a database of highly experienced and qualified valuers via the NAJ website.

Visit: www.naj.co.uk/consumer/help-and-advice

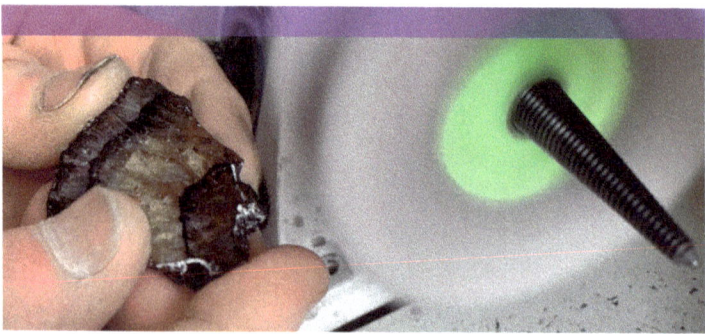

A demonstration – how to polish Blue John © *Kim Rix*

Top Ten

Questions to ask when buying jewellery

1. Do you have a return policy?
2. Is it covered by a warranty?
3. Does it come with an authenticity certificate?
4. Is it hallmarked?
5. What is the metal?
6. What are the gemstones?
7. Where was the piece made?
8. Can you give a valuation for insurance purposes?
9. How do I look after it?
10. Can you provide after care?

How to make a complaint

A little caution before you shop can save tears post purchase. It's safer to buy from retailers who have signed up to a recognised association and agreed to abide by a strict code of conduct. In the UK, we have several such associations – the National Association of Jewellers (NAJ) is one of the largest.

In Great Britain, you can buy safe in the knowledge that the Consumer Rights Act 2015 protects you if your purchases are not as described by the retailer, faulty, not fit for purpose or not of satisfactory quality. You can usually ask for a refund, repair or replacement.

Plan to put purchases between £100 and £30,000 on a credit card. Under Section 75 of the consumer credit act, your credit card company shares liability with the retailer on purchases between these limits. If there is a problem you are unable to resolve with the retailer, your credit card company will cover your loss.

Changing your mind

If your problem does not come under the Consumer Rights Act 2015, you will need to refer to the retailer's individual returns policy. Buying online in the UK gives you a 14-day cooling-off period, during which you can cancel or reject your order for a full refund without having to give a reason. Remember, though, that personalised jewellery or jewellery for piercings cannot be returned or exchanged unless it contravenes the Consumer Rights Act 2015. Before buying gemstones and jewellery here, it's a good idea to find out the shop's refund and exchange policy, in case you change your mind once you get back to the hotel room.

If things go wrong

Your first step should be to approach the retailer, explain the problem calmly and politely, and outline the action you would like the retailer to take. If you phone or visit in person, do remember to follow up with an email so that you have a written record of your dealings with each other. If you need to take your complaint further, you could seek help from the relevant trading association – but only if you've taken my advice and purchased from a member retailer!

After trying both approaches to no avail, it's time to turn to the law. In the UK, you could apply to have your case go through Small Claims – a relatively straightforward procedure for claims up to £10,000. Claims greater than £10,000 are more complicated and you will need proper legal advice.

A private collection of agates © Kim Rix

Lilies of the valley, white jasmin, fuchsia, snowdrops and cyclamen are represented in the Ashford black marble © *Kim Rix*

ESSENTIAL INFORMATION

Certificates of authenticity and grading reports

The value of a gemstone depends on several factors. At its most basic, the rule of thumb is this: the rarer, the bigger and the more naturally beautiful a gemstone is, the more it will be worth. The problem is that you cannot properly analyse a stone with the naked eye or even with a gemmologist's loupe (magnifying glass).

This is where the gem labs come in. In a gem lab, experts using high-tech equipment will be able to give you a lot of information about your stone. How much information you get depends on whether you want a certificate of authenticity or a grading report.

Certificate of authenticity
A certificate of authenticity is a written guarantee that your gemstone is what the seller says it is. It does not contain much specific detail about the stone. A certificate is really there to reassure you that you're getting a genuine gemstone and not a chunk of glass.

Grading report
A grading report gives a detailed analysis of a gemstone. It will provide you with a written assessment of your gemstone according to several criteria: carat weight, shape, size, colour description, clarity and the type of treatment it has undergone. A grading report can also tell you your gemstone's country of origin. This can have a bearing on the value of the gemstone because some countries have become associated with the quality of particular stones. Note that testing for origin can only be carried out on loose stones. If the gemstone has already been set into a piece of jewellery, it will need to be removed and then re-set after the test.

ESSENTIAL INFORMATION

Where to get your gemstones tested

London's Hatton Garden & Birmingham's Jewellery Quarter are the best places to access a gem lab in Britain. Three of the leading labs:

AnchorCert Gem Lab

The AnchorCert Gem Lab is Britain's leading gem lab. It's based at the Birmingham Assay Office, but you may also send gems to it for assessment via secure courier.

Visit: www.anchorcertgemlab.com

The Gem and Pearl Laboratory

Run by Stephen Kennedy, a gemmologist with experience of laboratory-based pearl and gem identification dating back to 1980. Next door to Hatton Garden, The Gem and Pearl Laboratory Limited was founded in 2003.

Visit: www.thegemlab.co.uk

Scottish pearl ring © Alistir Tate

Gemmological Certification Services

All the big auction houses use Gemmological Certification Services in New Bond Street, London.

Visit: www.gcslab.co.uk

BUYING GEMSTONES AND JEWELLERY IN **GREAT BRITAIN**

Jewellery shopping

Hatton Garden

Hatton Garden, in the London district of Holborn, is a commercial area famous as the centre of Britain's diamond trade. Diamond dealers and jewellers began to populate the area in the 1800s and today Hatton Garden is home to around 300 jewellery businesses, from independent shops to big names like De Beers. Hatton Garden is one of the best places in Britain to buy and sell gemstones and jewellery.

A list of jewellers:
www.hattongarden.com/directory

The Jewellery Quarter

Birmingham's Jewellery Quarter houses over 800 jewellers and independent retailers, making it the largest concentration of jewellers in Europe. It's a real treasure, described by English Heritage as 'a particular combination of structures associated with jewellery and metalworking which does not seem to exist anywhere else in the world.' In its heyday during the early 20th century, the Birmingham jewellery trade employed around 70,000 people. Many of today's makers are still working in original premises and using original machinery and tools.

Hatton Garden, famously known as London's jewellery quarter © Kim Rix

A list of jewellers: www.jewelleryquarter.net/the-directory

Importing and exporting

It is important to check your country's import and export regulations before buying in Great Britain as some items used in jewellery are subject to strict controls under the Convention of International Trade in Endangered Species (CITES). If you are caught out, your souvenir will be confiscated and you may also end up with a large fine.

The import/export items most regularly confiscated at UK customs are:

Fluorite from the Diana Maria Mine in Weardale, Bishop Auckland © Kim Rix

Elephant Ivory
It's currently legal to sell carved or worked antique ivory. In the UK, this is defined as ivory predating 1947. Exceptions exist for ivory worked between 1947 and 1990 with a government issued certificate.

Queen Conch Shells
Queen Conch Shells are found in the Carribean Sea and cannot be imported to the UK without a permit.

Sea Turtle Shells
Items made from the shells of endangered sea turtles are banned.

Coral
Many species of coral are endangered and there are rules about which you can bring into the UK.

Visit: www.gov.uk/guidance/cites-controls-import-and-export-of-protected-species

Horgabost, around the corner from Luskentyre on the Isle of Harris © *Kim Rix*

ESSENTIAL INFORMATION

www.gemstonedetective.com

Recommended books and useful links

Recommended reading by fellow gem enthusiasts:

Fluorite – by Trevor Ford

The book of Kells in Dublin – Trinity College

The Mabinogion – Britain's earliest prose stories, written in 12th-13th century Welsh.

Scottish Gemstones – by Newton Moore

Pearls – by Elizabeth Strack

Fluorspar in the North Pennines – Friends of Killhope

Derbyshire Black Marble – by John Michael Tomlinson and Trevor D Ford

Caves and Caverns of Peakland – by Crichton Porteous

Dolaucothi and Brunant – A Tale of Two Families in Wales – by David TR Lewis

The Gold Mines of Merioneth – by G W Hall

Useful links

Goldsmiths library and archives are for anyone researching jewellery, gold, silversmithing or family history.
Visit: www.thegoldsmiths.co.uk/craft/library-research

Mindat.org is an outreach project of the Hudson Institute of Mineralogy and is affiliated with the Friends of Mineralogy. Mindat.org aims to promote, support, protect and expand the collection of mineral specimens and to further the recognition of the scientific, economic and aesthetic value of minerals and collecting specimens.
Visit: www.mindat.org

ESSENTIAL INFORMATION

Gemdat.org is an online information resource dedicated to providing free gemmological information to all.
Visit: www.gemdat.org

The Society of British Jewellers
Visit: www.thesocietyofbritishjewellers.co.uk

British Geological Society has over 400 datasets in its care, including environmental monitoring data, digital databases, physical collections (borehole core, rocks, minerals and fossils), records and archives.
Visit: www.bgs.ac.uk

Aditnow has information on mine exploration and mining history, alongside photographs of mines.
Visit: www.aditnow.co.uk

10 times is an online list of upcoming trade shows and conferences, including gemstone and jewellery fairs and shows.
Visit: www.10times.com/unitedkingdom/gems-jewelry/tradeshows

British Tourist Board
Visit: www.visitbritain.com/gb/en

Festival of Geology
Visit: www.festivalofgeology.org.uk

The Mineralogical society
Visit: www.minersoc.org

The British Gold Panning Association
Visit: www.britishgoldpanningassociation.com

Take the ferry from Uig to Stornoway to visit the Isle of Lewis & Harris © *Kim Rix*

APPENDICES

Glossary

Adularescence An optical effect that makes a gemstone appear to glow from within. Moonstones exhibit adularescence.

Asterism An optical effect in which a six-rayed star appears to float just beneath the surface of the gem. Gemstones exhibiting asterism are given the name 'star'.

Bonny Bits Cubes of fluorite, used to make spar boxes.

Carat The unit used to measure the weight of a gemstone.

Certificate Confirmation that the gem in question is authentic.

Chatoyancy An optical effect in which a straight line appears to float just beneath the surface of the gem. Gemstones exhibiting chatoyancy are called 'cat's eye' stones.

CITES The Convention on International Trade in Endangered Species is an international treaty, which was signed in 1973 to protect animals and plants from over-exploitation. Almost 200 countries have now joined CITES.

Clarity The lack of inclusions (flaws) in a gemstone.

Corundum A very hard, transparent mineral. Ruby and sapphire are colour variations of corundum.

Crystal lattice dislocation	A disturbance in the arrangement of the stone's atoms.
Fluorescence	The ability of a gemstone to absorb ultraviolet light and emit it as visible light.
Fossilized resin	The viscous (thick, sticky) liquid which would run down the bark trapping insects.
Grading report	A detailed analysis of a gemstone's quality.
Heat treatment	A very old traditional method of improving the clarity of a gemstone. Not all gems can be treated in this way, but most sapphires are.
Homogenous	Has a uniform composition.
Hue	The colour of a stone.
Imitation	A stone that imitates a more expensive stone. An imitation stone might be a less valuable semi-precious stone or it might simply be coloured glass.
Inclusion	A fleck of material within a stone. A flaw.
Karat	Also spelled Carat, a measure of the fineness (i.e. purity) of gold. (24k gold is 99.95% pure).
Loupe	A small magnifying glass used to examine gems.
Lustre	The 'gleam' produced by light bouncing off the surface of a stone.

Metamorphic	Has undergone a physical change due to extreme heat and pressure.
Rough stone	A natural gemstone before it has been cut, or 'faceted'.
Saturation	The intensity of colour in a gemstone.
Simulant	Same as imitation. A cheap gemstone trying to look like a more valuable one.
Specific density	A number indicating how much heavier the gemstone is compared to an equal volume of water.
Spar Boxes	A free-standing glass-fronted case or box, encasing an arrangement of minerals found in the mines. ("Spar" is a contraction of "fluorspar".)
SSSI	Site of Special Scientific Interest. Rules may vary, but it's unlikely you will be allowed to remove anything of value from one of these.
Synthetic	A gemstone identical in structure to a mined gemstone, but formed in a lab rather than in the earth.
Tone	How light or dark a gemstone appears to be.

APPENDICES

Acknowledgements

I am grateful to the many kindred folk who generously contributed their time and expertise to speak with me at great length.

Above all, I appreciate the invaluable support and guidance provided throughout the research and writing process.

Special thanks to:
Jan Calligan, for her friendship and a VIP guided tour of Aberdeen.

Alan Greenlees, for sharing information about the Glasgow museums.

Alistir Tait, for his support and contribution with Scottish pearls.

Brian Shand, for talking to me at length about Portsoy marble.

David and Liz Hacker, for friendship and support with Blue John.

David Ifold, for explaining the legal and permission side of things, including Natural England and SSSI sites.

Sarah Steele, for the grand tour of Whitby and sharing her extensive knowledge of jet, including the identification of jet simulants.

Diana Bruce, for the tour of the Diana Maria mine and for making the introduction to David and Liz Hacker.

Gwern Gwynfil, for a memorable tour of the Welsh Gold Centre.

Paul Moreland, for showing me his splendid collection of agates and help with my research.

Matt Wall, for kindly introducing me to a number of useful contacts for this research.

Adam McIntosh, for kindly sharing images of Scottish jasper and other gemstones.

Lastly, my husband, Steven, for his input and proofreading.

About the author

Kim Rix is a professional photographer and qualified gemmologist (GIA). She travels extensively and has gathered a vast amount of the best local knowledge from her worldwide contacts.

Buying Gemstones & Jewellery in Great Britain is the eighth book in the *Gemstone Detective* series. Others in the series have been Sri Lanka, India, Australia, USA, Thailand, Myanmar and Worldwide.

Disclaimer: Kim Rix travelled around Great Britain (between lockdowns) in 2020 to gain insight into the marketplace with the intention of writing this book. Any resulting articles or publications should not be taken or used as an endorsement.

If we have made any errors in this book, please

 Forgive us

 Correct us

 Contact: kim@gemstonedetective.com

Connect with us

We would love you to leave a review of the book wherever you can – including Amazon, Google, Goodreads and our website.

 www.facebook.com/GemstoneDetective

 www.twitter.com/kimrix

 www.instagram.com/gemstone_detective

You can also sign up to receive our latest news and travels straight to your inbox via the website:

 www.gemstonedetective.com

Groups interested in arranging speaking engagements may contact the author via the website: www.gemstonedetective.com or by email at kim@gemstonedetective.com

Gemstone Tours with *Gemstone Detective* are escorted group tours. We visit the leading sources of colour gemstones, in search of ruby, sapphire, emerald, jade, opal and many others. For more information on booking a Gemstone Tour, please visit www.gemstonedetective.com/gemstone-tours

BUYING GEMSTONES AND JEWELLERY IN **GREAT BRITAIN**

Currently available

www.ingramcontent.com/pod-product-compliance
Lightning Source LLC
Chambersburg PA
CBHW041957080526
44588CB00021B/2780